101 Writers Short Blurb Examples

A selection of 101 'blurb' examples for fiction writers, all within 100 words or less, accompanied by a further 'distilled' example constructed in no more than one, single sentence.

By

QUENTIN COPE

COPYRIGHT & DISCLAIMER

Within this book some extracts from published novels may have been referred to or been described.

The authors and publishers have taken care to ensure that the information contained within this text is accurate and up to date and all references to services available are correct at time of publishing. However, readers are strongly advised to confirm this for themselves and neither the publisher nor the author will be responsible for any loss or damage of any nature associated with any reliance on the material or advice provided as part of this publication.

www.quentincope.co.uk

ISBN-10: 1496085760
ISBN-13: 978-1496085764

Available in Kindle from Amazon

FIRST EDITION

MIDNIGHT BLURB

T'was 'blurb' they said, he'd got it right,
Struggling, sweating, through the night,
His mind a blank, consumed by stress,
To be one hundred words … or less.
But then when daylight caught him low,
With simply nowhere else to go,
He came upon a thought profound,
Employ somebody next time round!

QPC

BOOKS BY QUENTIN COPE

Fiction - Thrillers

The Doksany Legacy
The Unicorn Conspiracy
The Geneveh Project
Rosalind
The Ludlum Prediction
Nostradamus: The Last Christmas

Non Fiction - Self Help - Reference

501 Writers Useful Phrases
501 "*More*" Writers Useful Phrases
501 Writers One-Liners
101Fiction Writing Tips
101 Writers Short Blurb Examples
A Novel Idea

Short Stories

The Rebels
The Terrorists

CONTENTS

Loose Subject Headings

Introduction

What is writers blurb?

There are many good books out there adequately describing the process of writing a 'blurb' for your next blockbuster and we include another book in this series *'101 Fiction Writing Tips'* amongst them. The dictionary definition of 'blurb' is as follows;

"A promotional description, as found on the jackets of books…"

So, that confirms it then. The size of the jacket or back cover of a paperback will more or less dictate the size, or number or words contained within your 'blurb' … and the average will probably be within the range of 200 to 300 words. Obviously compressing a storyline of some 60,000 words or more into an eye-catching two or three hundred is a major feat in its own right, but then there is the frustrating process of distilling it even further into possibly 100 words or less for promotional purposes. If you are pushing your work on social media, then often you have space for only one single sentence or a limited number of characters.

A good ‘blurb’ is the second ‘pull’ or ‘hook’ for a reader … with the first one being the cover image combined with a meaningful title. As the influence of EBook publishing increases, the self-published as well as the traditionally published author now relies very much on electronic book sales for a major part of their income.

With a limited amount of space available on a web page and with only a ‘thumbnail’ size image to wet your potential reader’s appetite, the ‘short blurb’ of up to 100 words becomes more and more important. It’s now recognized as part of the smart marketing process, inviting a browsing reader to delve more into your Web link, eventually opening up your book … and reading the first few pages.

Some fortunate individuals, along with many traditionally published authors, will have professionals employed to write ‘blurb’ for them, but the rest of us simply have to buckle down and get on with what is one of the most difficult processes of being a self-published writer. So, this little book will hopefully provide you with some useful assistance along the way by offering up 101 actual ‘blurbs’ written in short form and containing no more than 100 words.

They are loosely edited into ten different subject headings, or writer’s genre, with ten examples under each heading, except for the last one, where there are eleven. After each example, a further distillation of the same subject matter is provided, defined widely with a certain amount of writer's license, as a 'Single Sentence' … and both containing a word count as a confirmation of size.

So, how do I use them?

Well, by reading through the 'blurbs' that are nearest to the subject matter of your own work, you will be able to pick perhaps whole sentences, or perhaps a phrase or two, that describe similar situations to those you wish to emphasize in the blurb for your own story. Words in *italics* are highlighted as subject matter related to that particular blub and can therefore be abandoned when you modify the blurb or part of it as an individual sentence.

Reading through other authors 'blurb' for books containing similar subject matter to your own, with an idea to copying the general layout and construction, it's often difficult to get away from that particular author's description … no matter how much you try to re-invent it. Most writers have no problem putting many thousands of words together to produce an 'unputdownable' story … but those same writers find it often nearly impossible to write a blurb adequately revealing the pace and passion contained within their story … in 100 words or less!

The subject headings are described as ‘loose’ because that is what they are. If the book you wish to write ‘blurb’ for is say a ‘Romance’, don’t forget to have a look at some examples under other headings … as you may find just the phrase or sentence you are looking for requiring only a slight bit of ‘tweaking’!

An idea of the title connected to each blurb example is also provided as the blurb, a cover image and the title of a book are nearly always linked as part of the major ‘hook’ for the reader. These titles are only meant to relate to the blurb content and not to any published work by any particular author.

Hopefully, within these few thousand words, you will find what you are looking for which are hopefully examples of snappy, eye catching blurbs providing an immediate ‘hook’ to many of your potential readers. None of the examples shown here, to the best knowledge of the author, are actual blurbs from published novels or other writers work. They are all original, written by the author and first offered in this publication. Therefore you can ‘cut and paste’ to use any part of them … or all of them without any editing requirements or infringement of any copyright connected to the blurb examples described.

Action & Adventure

Instinct for Survival

Short Blurb: For *her*, the 'Ides of March' were coming a month early and now it was time to 'beware' as the confrontation ahead may take more from *her* than *she* has left to give. Is a strong survival instinct the only adrenalin required to conquer *her* fear of the future? Whoever admits to it means someone inevitably has to come second in a race of absolute survival. You will simply not be able to put this one down … until the singularly surprising finale! (83 Words)

Single Sentence: In a race for survival, someone always has to come second, unless of course an adrenalin driven confrontation can somehow be turned to a surprising advantage! (26 Words)

When the Devil Returns

Short Blurb: When the comfortable world of retirement for *Ex-CIA Agent Tom Smith* is shattered by the cruel and sadistic actions of a former adversary, it's time to leave a shattered family behind and face *his* innermost fears. Someone will have to die. (41 Words)

Single Sentence: When a retired *CIA agent* is reactivated in the search for a sadistic former adversary, someone will inevitably have to die! (21 Words)

Essential Extraction

Short Blurb: An embarrassing covert military mission in the headlines, a failed plan and the International consequences of a political cover-up, kick-start the involvement of *Tom Warren*, Ex-Navy Seal and mercenary recruiter. It means getting back into the *South American* state of *Argona* again, a place of total anarchy and a law laid down with relish by brutal drug baron *Jose Fernandez*. The *CIA* want him back in *America* … *Tom Warren* is sent to get him. Failure is not an option! (80Words)

Single Sentence: When *Tom Warren* get's involved, the word 'mercenary' takes on a new meaning and brutal drug baron *Jose Fernandez* is about to have his travel plans rearranged … for good! (30 Words)

A Race for Freedom

Short Blurb: When an Archaeological dig in the heart of *North Africa* becomes a scene of carnage after an attack by fanatical religious terrorists, two captured survivors need to somehow avoid a ritual beheading. *Dr Clancy Wagner* and his beautiful assistant *Mary Brown* manage to escape their captors under cover of darkness. Who will be first in a race to the coast and possible freedom for the *two* adventurers? With a twist in the tail, this gripping, enveloping story will leave you breathless. (81 Words)

Single Sentence: Two archaeologists, the suffocating heat of a wild, unruly *North African* state and a band of marauding, fanatical religious terrorists, combine in this gripping story of capture, bloody ancient ritual and eventual escape. (33 Words)

The Cavendish Discovery

Short Blurb: Its 2014, but events that took place in 1914, one hundred years ago, will force *Bill Winston* the think again about his impending marriage to wealthy heiress *Fiona Cavendish.* Will the past of *Fiona's* grandfather send *Winston* on an adventure to uncover a miscarriage of justice, an investigation that could be his undoing, perhaps even his untimely end? As each chapter unfolds, the mystery deepens until finally the truth is revealed, but will a reluctant *Fiona Cavendish* eventually be able to squarely face her many personal demons? (87 Words)

Single Sentence: It happened a hundred years ago, but if a search for the truth by adventurer *Bill Winston* is successful, will wealthy heiress *Fiona Cavendish* be able to face the multi-faceted demons of a dubious past? (35 Words)

Retribution Denied

Short Blurb: Sent into a war torn Iraq, two *ex-navy seals* are looking for something. But what … and who has sent them there? The *CIA* doesn't want to know, but other governmental forces are at work and so the hunt begins. With the help of a serving *American* military officer, they find the first clue to uncovering a massacre where thirty six soldiers died … butchered by a *Taliban* leader looking to avenge the death of his only son at the hands of a special forces hit squad. Making a promise maybe one thing, but keeping it is another! (98 Words)

Single Sentence: A massacre of US soldiers by an embittered Taliban leader and two ex-navy seals on the hunt for the perpetrator, lead to a situation where the hunters suddenly becomes the hunted in an unexpected check-mate finale. (36 Words)

Conspiracy to Deceive

Short Blurb: What is he doing in the middle of the *Nevada desert* wearing literally no clothes, with no means of transport and no memory of how on earth he got there? *Tom Wyatt* is a geologist who has spent his life looking for oil, but now he is looking for something completely different. The last thing he remembers is kissing his wife goodnight in Pittsburgh, but here he is now, sitting half dressed in the desert … so how many days ago was that? The dust trail in the distance … heading in his direction may hold the chilling answer. (99 Words)

Single Sentence: Being left exposed and half clothed in the middle of the *Nevada desert* does nothing to indicate to geologist *Tom Wyatt* how he got there … but perhaps someone responsible for stirring up the quickly approaching dust cloud has the unsettling answer? (42 Words)

Captured in the Caribbean

Short Blurb: It started out as an adventure for *Maureen Stillsby*, a fun adventure that would earn her and her friend *Caroline* a couple of thousand dollars and a free holiday in *Costa Rica*. It wasn't so funny now. The overcrowded prison cell stank of urine and body odour, and they had known it as home for over a week. Will these two adventurous teenagers from *Middle America* be able to survive the lustful interest of other inmates and the violent attention of the prison guards? A story of harrowing misfortune that could easily happen to you and is genuinely un-put-down-able! (99 Words)

Single Sentence: Two adventurous teenage girls from *Middle America*, a seemingly cheap *Caribbean* holiday and a stinking *Costa Rica* prison cell are all part of the wallpaper in this harrowing story of anguish and violence in a world of International drug smuggling and deep seated corruption. (44 Words)

Too Hot to Hide

Short Blurb: A fast car, a card with unlimited credit and a yearning to have fun is the reward for hard work and a place at *Harvard*. However, two days into his holiday *Chuck* is on the run from ruthless gangsters without a sense of humour, desperate for a conversation. Whatever he saw, whoever he spoke to on that fateful *Friday* in *Atlanta*, he could not remember, but with a failed kidnapping attempt behind him, a bleeding bullet wound in his left shoulder, *Chuck* didn't want to hang around to find out. However things could get worse … and that's for sure! (100 Words)

Single Sentence: Something odd must have happened in *Atlanta,* but *Chuck* couldn't remember what it was … and now on the run, escaping from a kidnapping attempt by the skin of his teeth and a bleeding bullet wound in his shoulder, he is convinced it must have been important. (47 Words)

Search for the Enemy Within

Short Blurb: When the *Chief Security Officer* at a top secret facility in *Michigan* is murdered, no one can figure out what he died of. When *Head of Project Development, Peter Whitehead* attempts to contact the victim's family … they have all disappeared and now certain individuals in the *White House* are taking more than a passing interest in the situation? In the middle of a cold war, the enemy is considered to be *Russian* … but what if the real enemy is much closer to home. An explosive beginning … an unbelievable ending … the pace will leave you breathless! (99 Words)

Single Sentence: Murder at a top secret US research facility; the victims family vanishing and now *White House* heavy's on the case … Peter *Whitehead, Head of Project Development* wants to know if the enemy is really a few thousand miles away … or residing in the office next door! (48 Words)

Crime & Criminals

The Two Billion Dollar Break-in!

Short Blurb: Breaking out of prison was understandable … breaking in was not. However … *Harry Sharkov* needed the knowledge of one man, and one man only to ensure the biggest planned heist in *US* history became a success. A shipment of *two billion dollars in gold* was about to leave *Fort Worth* for the *Saudi Arabian capital of Riyadh*, but with the help of incarcerated ace safe code cracker *Tommy*, *Harry* planned to ensure it never got there. Could anything conceivably go wrong? Well … getting a reluctant *Tommy* out of the notorious *Rikers Island* facility would be a good start! (100 Words)

Single Sentence: A planned prison break-in means that someone has surely got it wrong … but not with two billion dollars worth of gold hanging on the end of a possibly disappointing result for the central bank of *Saudi Arabia!* (38 Words)

The Killer Communications

Short Blurb: *Detective Lieutenant Rick Stanley* knew the person responsible for some gruesome deaths on his patch was sending a message of some kind … but what? His colleagues, and especially his boss, *Captain O'Brien*, thought differently … and they were becoming frustrated with lack of progress on the four individual murders. When body number five turns up, *Rick* is taken off the case … but now he has a clue, the message has been received …and he is determined to catch the serial killer, who he now knows is one of his own! But can he prove it? (97 Words)

Single Sentence: A serial killer on the loose has become a political 'hot potato' and when *Detective Lieutenant Rick Stanley* is removed from the case he turns his attention closer to home, only to discover the killer's identity … and one he will find difficult to prove! (45 Words)

They Called Him Lucky

Short Blurb: *Tony (Lucky) Cypriani* was a 'not so bright' bank robber, not a petty thief handbag dipper; but needs must when times get hard. So when he comes up with a wallet, a phone and a little black book dipped from a smartly dressed gent at a busy *Penn Station*, he's unaware his life is to change dramatically … and not for the better! The predator is now the prey. Tony and his ill-gotten gains become wanted property. He doesn't know why, but on the run for weeks, he meets someone who can tell him. Now he really is in trouble! (100 Words)

Single Sentence: One wallet snatch too many, a little black book and a phone that never rings leaves a 'not so bright' *Tony (Lucky) Cypriani* wondering what the hell was happening … until, on the run to nowhere, someone unexpectedly tells him. (40 Words)

The Cruel Web of the Comforting Spider

Short Blurb: When well presented *con-artist Bertram*, and wealthy *middle aged widow Fiona* book into the upmarket *Shires Hotel*, they are both there for different reasons … or so one would think. However, they quickly become involved and *Bertram* starts to groom the outwardly gushing *Fiona* with a view to stealing all her money. Little does he know that she is in fact the predator in this new partnership, which literally turns into a cold, emotionless series of criminal adventures targeting the wealthy and the unwise … until one day? (88 Words)

Single Sentence: When an experienced *con-artist* and a *middle aged widow* meet, they embark on a series of daring criminal escapades designed to fleece the wealthy and line their own pockets … until something unpredictable happens to turn their criminal lifestyle on its head! (42 Words)

Disaster in Detroit

Short Blurb: It was not meant to go off … but it did, and one man died. Robbing the headquarters of the biggest *drug dealers in Detroit* was not a bright idea, but now it was too late. *Delroy and Sylvester* packed quickly, leaving for a new life in *Florida* with their ill-gotten, criminal gains. When it happened, it was unexpected … a confrontation in a bar, leaving them on the run again … until they meet *FBI Agent Thomas.* What he wants is against the code … but they have no choice in a particularly one sided trust scenario. (97 Words)

Single Sentence: An accidental shooting, whilst foolishly attempting to rob a drug dealing headquarters in *Detroit,* is a mistake that will inevitably cost *Delroy and Sylvester* their lives … unless the unusual opportunity provided by gritty, straight talking *FBI Agent Thomas* … can be trusted. (43 Words)

The Hotshots Predicament

Short Blurb: They were just kids … running errands for small time dealers on street corners. But they grew up into the most feared gang of merciless criminals in *Boston. Police Chief Robertson* was elected on the promise of eliminating the *'Hotshots' gang* and cleaning up the streets for his upper class voters. He meant what he said, but the methods used were at best a little crude and unconventional and for a while, everyone turned the other way. So when the

'Hotshots' fought back, no-one was even mildly prepared for what was to happen next! (94 Words)

Single Sentence: They started out as kids making deliveries and ended up leading the most feared drug dealing gang in *Boston*, a town that new *Police Chief Robertson* was bent on cleaning up, but without knowing what mayhem the *'Hotshots'* had in store for him, and his collection of upper class voters! (50 Words)

A Highly Successful Robbery Mystery

Short Blurb: It was a robbery, pure and simple. A well planned and well executed *robbery* taking the *armoured vehicle* driver and crew completely by surprise. What they didn't reckon on was what was inside the van when they opened it up. Was it valuable? Could they actually sell it? What the hell was it doing there? Only one man could help with the mystery and that's how *Frankie Large* became involved. Yes, he knew its worth. Yes, it could be sold … but then he told them who it belonged to. Dear oh dear! (93 Words)

Single Sentence: A well planned and executed *armoured vehicle robbery* left them holding something … something seemingly intangible, something that could perhaps be very valuable … and when *Frankie Large* provided the answer to the mystery … every single one of them wished he hadn't! (43 Words)

Final Confrontation

Short Blurb: *Tommy Rodriquez* is a loner. He robs alone, does his time alone and drinks alone. So when a beautiful young *Mexican* girl enters his life, he's initially cautious but then she becomes part of his world and an accomplice in a life of crime. They are living a fast paced, adrenalin fuelled existence for three glorious years until one day, in a street shootout, the girl dies. *Tommy* embarks on a grief fuelled robbing spree that must be brought to an end. *Lieutenant Sanchez* is given the job and when the two men come face to face, something unexpected happens. (100 Words)

Single Sentence: In a *Bonny and Clyde* style existence, *Tommy Rodriquez* and his beautiful *Mexican* female partner generate fear wherever they go when one day, his girl is shot dead in front of him and he embarks of a bloody trail of vengeance … until he comes face to face with *Lieutenant Sanchez* … a man on a mission who can make unexpected things happen! (63 Words)

Dilemma of the Data Dealers

Short Blurb: The set of *bank data files* on the memory stick in *Billy Baldwin's* pocket were his ticket south to a land of sun, cheap booze and good looking women. The man he was meeting in ten minutes guaranteed it. He would buy each of the *5,000 stolen personal files* from *Billy* for $50.00 each … at least that's what he said on the phone. The feel of a .38 gun barrel against *Billy's* ear, however, would force him to change his mind. Someone wanted what was on one of those files … and they weren't about to pay for it. (100 Words)

Single Sentence: *Billy Baldwin* calculated a set of several thousand *stolen bank data files* should have been his ticket to a life of leisure in the sun, but the unwelcome feel of a .38 gun barrel in his ear told him that the 'buyer' would not be happily parting with any money today. (51 Words)

The Mouse-men Robberies

Short Blurb: It was what the police called a *'white collar crime'*, but *Detective Roberts* of *LAPD* called it simply 'crime'! Three million dollars stolen 'on-line' was still three million … and he was determined to catch the perpetrators. But what would *Roberts* do when he found that one of the attic computer criminals involved was his own *son*? How could he send the others down and keep his *boy* out of it? There was work to be done … but would he get away with it? (85 Words)

Single Sentence: *LAPD Detective Roberts* was on the trail of a well organised gang of successful 'on-line' thieves … in a big way, but when he found out his *son* was one of them, he desperately needed a foolproof plan to send the others down, keep his *boy* out of it … and then get away with it! (55 Words)

Fantasy Themes

Justice Sword – The Final Reprisal

Short Blurb: *Prince Hagar* awaits trial for treason in the notorious *Norwith* prison whilst his brother languishes in the dungeons of *Greyshere Castle*. His whole family are being hunted down by the powerful *Celtana clan,* ruling the north of the country with an iron fist. On his way to the trial, being dragged through the streets by his captors, a sword is thrown to him from the crowd … the magical *'Justice Sword'* given to him by his grandfather when he was a young boy. By simply grasping it, his shackles fall away … now the bloodbath would begin. (97 Words)

Single Sentence: When the magical *'Justice Sword'* is thrown to *Prince Hagar* as he is dragged through the streets, on his way to trial for treason; simply holding it make his shackles fall away … releasing him to free his dying bother in the dungeons of *Greyshere Castle* … and exact a bloody justice on all who stand in his way. (59 Words)

Prince Algar and King of the Grobes

Short Blurb: In the underworld of *Hegenot,* all is at peace, as it has been for several hundred years.

However, the appearance of a stranger, from a land beyond the forest, causes disunity when he tells of threats from the neighbouring *Grobes*. He claims to be a *wizard* who will help the *Hegenot's* to win a war against their old enemies … but is he telling the truth? Determined not to be tricked, *Prince Algar* sets of on a quest to confront the king of the *Grobes*, but it is a journey fraught with danger along with some surprising discoveries. (98 Words)

Single Sentence: *Prince Algar* does not believe the *wizard,* a stranger who suddenly appears in the peaceful underworld of the *Hegenot,* telling stories of possible war with his old enemies, and so sets off on a journey of danger and discovery … to confront his neighbour, *King of the Grobes.*(48 Words)

The Demon and the Prince of Secrets

Short Blurb: *Lady Guinevere* holds a secret she dare not tell her husband and her King until she is born of a son. She is about to give birth to a child that *Court Wizard Argonne* confirms is a boy, but then is kidnapped by agents of the despotic and powerful *Prince of the Zealanders* for ransom. Imprisoned in a high tower, *Lady Guinevere* delivers a boy child; now the secret can be revealed and the power of the *Black Demon* released to vent his wrath on all the enemies of the new born prince with frightening consequences. (96 Words)

Single Sentence: A daring kidnap and imprisonment of the betrothed of a king … someone about to deliver a child, leaves the *Prince of the Zealanders* pleased with his ransom plan, until the birth of a boy prince unveils a secret and releases the Black Demon who will exact fearful vengeance all the new born Prince's perceived enemies … with frightening consequences! (60 Words)

Fantastic Abandonment

Short Blurb: It must simply be fantasy … a dream of little consequence; it could not possibly be real. *Mary Greenhough* is a solid, sensible woman; a high flying financial executive and not given to anything near a 'flight of fantasy' in her busy working schedule. So why is she here … on this wondrously deserted beach, half naked, in the company of this unbelievably handsome young man; waves crashing against silvered rocks as they both sip chilled champagne. She appears to be in another world … and this first instinct is about to be proved correct. So … what happens next? (100 Words)

Single Sentence: Solid, reliable and successful financial executive *Mary Greenhough* is either having a dream or is actually living out a fantasy, sipping champagne, mostly naked on a tropical beach with an unbelievably handsome young man, who will need to provide the answer to the singularly intriguing question of … what happens next? (51 Words)

In The Name of the Beast

Short Blurb: When two powerful *12th Century Alchemists* combine forces to undermine the power of the *King,* they know they are on dangerous ground. But the country is gradually falling into total bankruptcy as the *King and his Princes* make more and more demands on the landowners for higher and higher taxes, feeding an increasingly hedonistic royal lifestyle. They must release a *beast* on the land, an invincible *beast* ready to *smite all royal personages* without fear or favour. But what happens when that job is done … who will the beast come after next? (93 Words)

Single Sentence: With a once influential country collapsing into economic ruin, two *powerful 12th Century Alchemists* join together to release a *beast* on the land that will rid it of a corrupt, hedonistic royalty … but have they thought of what is to happen to an invincible beast when that job is done? (51 Words)

Search for the Shield of Aramar

Short Blurb: It is the golden *Shield of Aramar* the *Crusaders* seek in a land ruled by the tough fighting *Moors.* Its magical powers will allow the *Knights Templar* to defeat the evil *Imad of Damascus* and thereby free the *Byzantine lands* forever. When they meet a soothsayer on the road south from *Constantinople*, they learn the whereabouts of the shield … and something about the three headed *Beast of Calamnar* who guards it. Along with courage, will they need only the mystic and his knowledge of spells to continue their quest, or something more substantial? (94 Words)

Single Sentence: In order to capture the mythical golden *Shield of Aramar* in the land of the tough fighting *Moors*, a determined group of *Knights Templar*, with assistance from a mystic they meet on the road from *Constantinople*, need to get past the three headed *Beast of Calamnar* and may perhaps need something more substantial than simply great courage … and a few soothsayer's spells! (63 Words)

Torment of the Vampire Hunter

Short Blurb: When *vampires* sleep, others search for them, especially if they inhabit the *central European region of Transvakia. Doctor Karl Ironakov* is a professional *vampire* hunter. He hunts them by day … and they hunt him by night. Who will survive this cat and mouse game of a possibly superior supernatural force versus the strength of will of just one man? With action building to a tormenting climax, eventually the adversaries come face to face at *Castle Dronesburg.* But will there be an unanticipated resolution to what appears, on the face of it, to be a deadly one sided confrontation? (99 Words)

Single Sentence: When determined *vampire* hunter *Doctor Karl Ironakov* comes face to face with his arch nemesis and life-long adversary at *Castle Dronesburg in Tranvakia,* it appears to be a one-sided confrontation that only a resilient, ancient supernatural power can win … until an unanticipated resolution is suddenly made possible. (48 Words)

The Sinister Spirit of Salytal

Short Blurb: *Salytal,* in a need to save his son from everlasting slavery makes the supreme sacrifice, and now lives in another world with what he has become. Abandoned by those on a physical plane, he must discover the secret of his own vile darkness if he is to stop the *Black Lord* from annihilating what is left of humanity. Battling to be released from the powers consuming him, *Salytal* searches for a weakness in the *Black Lord's* armour, but in order to prevail, he must find a way to turn his own sinister spirit into the deliverance of the human race. (100 Words)

Single Sentence: Abandoned by those on a physical plane, *Salytal* searches for a weakness in the metaphysical armour of the *demon Black Lord*, but has somehow to direct his own sinister spirit toward the deliverance of the human race before he can stand against *the demon* ... and release his own tortured soul. (51 Words)

The Ways of the Wizard

Short Blurb: With *Targonia* on the verge of a civil uprising led by the *Wizard Unigar, Rhanbar* searches to find a new, more powerful source of magic in order to impose his will on the warring factions. In desperation, he makes an arrangement with the *Caliph of Dargon*, and strengthened with a power he believes that not even Unigar can match, Rebus embarks on a journey to the farthest limits of the land. But in the final confrontation will the power of *Rebus* and the *Caliph of Dargon* be enough? Not if the wily *Wizard Unigar* has his way! (96 Words)

Single Sentence: Will *Rhanbar* and the devious magic practised by the powerful *Caliph of Dargon*, be enough to thwart the evil plans for a civil uprising in the tempestuous land of *Targonia*, led by the *Wizard Unigar* ... or will the wily one win in a final confrontation that may not be destined to go *Rhanbar's* way! (55 Words)

A Shifting Conclusion

Short Blurb: *Donna Keely* knows about *shifters* ... she is one! Being the only human she knows of in a *Wolf pack* has provided certain challenges, to the point of painful rejection by the pack. In a quest for survival she takes work with a mainly human company. When the human owner asks *Donna* to assist in finding the person behind some important missing company documents, she is reticent. However, little does she realize who it will eventually pit her against … in a life or death struggle with another cast out member of her own pack? (95 Words)

Single Sentence: Being a cast out human in a close grouped wolf pack leaves *shifter Donna* working for a human company and searching for a thief, until the pressure racks up when she reluctantly comes face to face, in a life or death struggle with the surprising perpetrator … another cast out member of her own pack! (55 Words)

Historical Drama

The Winslow Legacy

Short Blurb: In the wild slums of late *nineteenth century Chicago*, one young boy has a dream. *Tom Winslow*'s dream will take him away from his place of torment and make him a *wealthy trader* at the age of thirty. Unmarried and desperate to create the warm family life he never had, he sets out on a journey to find a wife. When he does, his life is gloriously complete until she is cruelly taken in *child birth*. Can *Tom* ever truly connect with his surviving son through the heartbreak and profound feelings of guilt at the death of this boys' mother? (100 Words)

Single Sentence: A touching rags to riches story set in tough, *nineteenth century Chicago* ends cruelly when entrepreneur *Tom Winslow's wife* is taken from him in childbirth … leaving him desperate in his efforts to try and connect with his surviving son, through a veil of guilt and personal recrimination. (48 Words)

Ride to Retribution

Short Blurb: The railway was coming. It was unstoppable. It would have to go through the *estate* of

Thomas Filsbury ... or so they said. Money could not do it ... so what would it take for *Thomas* to see sense. With his farms being decimated, one by one; his tenants terrorised and livestock being slaughtered, he will have to give in. There is nowhere to turn for justice in *eighteenth century England* ... until one day a stranger appears who possesses strength, cunning and skills enough to right some wrongs ... and make the purveyors of misery pay dearly! (98 Words)

Single Sentence: In the face of massive and cruel intimidation, *Thomas Filsbury* still provides a firm 'No' to the new fangled railway carving its way across his estate in *eighteenth century England* ... until, one day, a stranger appears who is possessed of skills and cunning enough to turn the tables on the faceless industrialists ... making them pay dearly! (58 Words)

The Keeper

Short Blurb: To *Billy Braggs*, war was guaranteed money ... money for anything ... money for everything. It's *1917* and the *back streets of London* are a dangerous place to be caught sightseeing. *Black market entrepreneur Billy* caught on early to the significant need for *soap* in the *war torn British Empire* ... and so has cornered the market in it. However, he makes a significant 'slip' when he employs the voluptuous and educated book-keeper

Molly, to look after his accounts. Little does he know, but she plans to look after much, much more than that! (94 Words)

Single Sentence: *Billy Braggs,* successful black marketer in a dismal *1917 London*, has it all and is looking for even more when he employs voluptuous and well educated book-keeper *Molly* … not knowing that she plans to look after a lot more than just his books! (44 Words)

Rise of the Unchained

Short Blurb: *New Orleans* in *1840*; *slave trading capital* of the world. *Stanley Frazier;* master slave breeder who has created a fortune by the study of his craft. Haughty and disparaging of all others, he is disliked within southern society, rarely making a visit to the *Orleans* slave market, which he owns. Ripe for bringing down, one man, *Moses Odwaba,* his long serving 'trusty' is waiting for the moment. But is he resolute enough to free over six hundred fit, sexually starved young men to wreak havoc on a delicate, unsuspecting society and take down the man who calls himself their 'father'? (100 Words)

Single Sentence: It's the dark days of *1840,* in a *New Orleans* where slave breeder and trader *Stanley Frazier,* is disliked by many, but never more than *Moses Odwaba,* a long serving *'trusty'* who is planning to release over six hundred sexually starved, fit young men on an unsuspecting *Orleans* society and finally take down the man who boasts of being their 'father'. (61 Words)

The Saving of Juliet

Short Blurb: Life for *Juliet Swan* was difficult, but stimulating in *1920's New York.* Her father, an upright *nineteenth century citizen*, saw no future in a fast living, drunken jitterbugging society and therefore a rebellious *Juliet* was forced to make a choice. She made one; running off with an exciting young *piano player* of weak character and no future. Eventually, lack of substance would take its toll, until years later her father rescues her from the filth and squalor of a *south side drug den.* This is the heartbreaking story of how she got there and the compassion that eventually saved her. (100 Words)

Single Sentence: A young, vivacious and headstrong *Juliet Swan* had it all in *1920's New York*, but little did her father know he would have to rescue her, years later, from the filth and squalor of a *south side drug den* ... and this is the shatteringly heartbreaking story of how he got there. (52 Words)

The First Forester

Short Blurb: The first rays of crisp, spring sunlight broke through the *Canadian forest* darkness to light up the rough carved, timber sign of the *Hudson Bay*

Company, nailed to the door of the sturdy timber shelter built by *Jean le Charmon.* This is the story of how he arrived at the *Ross River Trading Post Number three in 1671* as one of the company's first employees … and how he survived the next forty torturous years there as master of all around him. (82 Words)

Single Sentence: A simple but gripping story about one mentally and physically resilient man who had the courage in 1671 to carve a trading route through the *Canadian* outback, build one of the first *Hudson Bay Company* trading posts at *Ross River* … and live there long enough to call it home! (50 Words)

The Devonshire Generations

Short Blurb: Telling a story spanning *four generations* from *1860 to 1960,* the rags to riches life of the *Devonshire clan*, reveals a whole range of emotions, upsets, trials and tribulations that will make some stronger … and completely destroy others. How *Samuel Devonshire* became the powerful *Philadelphia* newspaper magnate that he eventually did, was not without its mystery. However, a generation or two later, the family hold ambitions far greater than media control of just one or two states … they are looking at the making of a President … and political control of the whole damn country! (97 Words)

Single Sentence: The building of a rich and powerful media dynasty leaves the *Devonshire clan*, in *1960's America*, controlling something more than the minds of a nation, now they want to make sure the *President of the United States of America* is one of their own as well … confirming a possibly tenuous political domination of the most powerful country on earth. (60 Words)

Poachers Choice

Short Blurb: If anyone wanted to achieve little more than survival as a lowly farm hand on a *country estate in 1910,* they would have few choices. *Poaching* was, however, one of them … and *Robert Cape* was good at it. He was also good at capturing the attention of young ladies in the village and some others, such as estate owner and landlord, *Rupert De Winter*, were not impressed. His downfall was a shooting incident, at night, in the woods where *De Winter's head gamekeeper* was killed. With *Robert Cape* on the run, was this proof of his guilt? (98 Words)

Single Sentence: A shooting incident, in woods, at night, leaving a *head gamekeeper* dead was enough to send well known local poacher and admirer of young ladies, *Robert Cape*, on the run in *1910* … but was this really proof of his guilt? (41 Words)

The Petticoat Spy Predicament

Short Blurb: During the *American Civil War*, being caught on the wrong side meant you were a spy and could be shot, but there were some in southern society that could travel north with impunity and gather good intelligence by simply engaging in polite party conversation. For *Leticia Howard* however this was not enough and she was caught in possession of some very compromising documents. What would *US Intelligence Colonel Travers* do with her? With some surprising twists and turns, this is the story of her amazing survival and an even more extraordinary finale! (92 Words)

Single Sentence: Regular traveller and socialite *Leticia Howard* was a spy for the *Confederates* during the *American Civil War*, and when caught, had to admit it, leaving *US Intelligence Colonel Travers* some interesting choices with respect to her survival … and eventually, a most unexpected outcome! (44 Words)

The Righteous Revolutionary

Short Blurb: The second *Industrial Revolution* was in full swing and in *1840*, the town of *Chicago* benefitted more than most. With *steam engines replacing horses*, more work was being done with less labour … and this was where the problems began. The *industrialists* demanded efficiency … and laid-off workers demanded food. Eventually the two would clash, led by one barely educated man who finally raised an army of angry workers bent on demolition of the machinery gradually destroying their lives. This is the story of that one, brave and charismatic individual who demanded justice … and eventually received it! (98 Words)

Single Sentence: During an Industrial Revolution, where machines replaced men and laid-off workers were left to starve in 1840's Chicago, one barely educated individual would rise up and lead an army of angry young men, bent on destroying the machinery that was denying them work and dignity … and this is their harrowing story. (52 Words)

Mystery & Suspense

A History of Darkness

Short Blurb: It was only a week … but it could have been a year since *Chantelle Du Bois* had become involved in a mystery now ruling her every waking moment. Who was the scruffily dressed old man who kept appearing, then equally as quickly disappearing from her life? Was this something to do with her *father's past,* a *well respected diplomat* who had simply ceased to exist on that fateful Friday two years previously? She had to find out … but taking a step into the darkness of her *father's past*, alone, may be the last thing she would ever do! (100 Words)

Single Sentence: *Chantelle Du Bois*, daughter of a *diplomat father* who has mysteriously disappeared, needs to know who the scruffy old man is who keeps popping in and out of her life … but to do so, she may be required to delve into her *father's past* … and that could be a dark place to go … a very dark place indeed! (61 Words)

An Impossible State of Affairs

Short Blurb: It was only politics … until people started dying! *Vice President Williams* knew there was something much more deeply seated, much more dangerous and infectious in the *White House underworld affairs of state* than the *Chief of Staff* was admitting. Was there anyone at all he could trust … or was he alone in his mission to get to the bottom of what was happening … and stay alive himself ? (71 Words)

Single Sentence: With secretive, underworld affairs of state undermining the *White House* and a *Chief of Staff* remaining tight lipped, people are dying and *Vice President Williams* feels it's time to take action … knowing he needs to get to the bottom of it all, but will he be alone … and has he got what it takes to stay alive himself? (60 Words)

The Berlin Code Mystery

Short Blurb: In the final throes of *World War II,* a top secret raid on a *Berlin inner defence headquarters* by a specialist *US Ranger* unit uncover and retrieve a set of undecipherable code books. However, fifteen years later, the *Russian military in East Berlin* suddenly start using the codes for radio transmissions to Moscow. What is going on … and what are the transmissions linked to? *Colonel Robertson*, one of the original *Rangers* involved in the *1945* raid, is despatched to find out … but is the frighteningly chilling mystery more than one man can handle? (95 Words)

Single Sentence: Twenty year old *World War II* cipher codes being used by *the Russians* cause a stir at the *Pentagon* and sending a specialist such as *Colonel Robertson* to find out what is going on may not have been a good idea … especially when the mystery deepens and nothing but a chilling end is in sight for all involved! (59 Words)

Agent in the Mirror

Short Blurb: She is having a love affair. She thinks her husband knows nothing of it. However, *Sir John Witham, British Secret Service*, not only knows about his wife's lover, he also knows where he has trained in *Russia,* which department of the *GRU* he works for and what his mission is. Now, it's a waiting game until someone makes a move allowing the *Russian* to be turned and sent back as a double agent. The problem is, the *GRU* know more about *Sir John* than he thinks … and the high stakes game of chess is about to begin! (98 Words)

Single Sentence: Can the love affair embarked upon by the wife of a senior *Secret Service grandee* be turned to an advantage, sending a *Russian spy* back as one of their own … or will the secret life of *Sir John Witham* play some part in the possible downfall of such a daring plan? (52 Words)

The Zermatt Trigger

Short Blurb: Murder on the exclusive *Swiss ski slopes of Zermatt* kick-starts a chain of events forcing *French DGSE operative, Francoise Chelan*, to chase all over *Europe* in search of a group of *Algerian terrorists* planning to assassinate his country's *President*. He knows the day, the time and the place but not how. Are the *Algerian group* much cleverer than first thought? Will one careful, methodical and dedicated intelligence officer work it out in time? With the *Russians* and *British* watching very carefully in the wings, an opportunity could be created to destroy the troubled *European Union* and create political world chaos! (100 Words)

Single Sentence: *Zermatt* and its exclusive *ski slopes* is the backdrop to a murder that may have sensitive political implications with the involvement of *Algerian terrorists,* a planned assassination attempt on the *French President* and only one determined *French security operative Francoise Chelan* left to work it all out! (47 Words)

A Hopeless Project

Short Blurb: When *CIA agent Jon Kincaid* is dragged from his bed in the early hours, drugged and transported to a deserted *Venezuelan island*, his boss on *Project Hope* sets up a massive manhunt. The orders are that *top secret Project Hope* must not be compromised in any way and if necessary, *Kincaid* must be eliminated. But … the best laid plans of 'mice and men' can go wrong … and this one did … big time! (75 Words)

Single Sentence: A kidnapped *CIA agent* left on a deserted *Venezuelan island*; a possibly compromised *top secret project* and a plan that was destined to go wrong from the very start will leave you wanting more from the very moment you meet a tough, resolute and fearless *Jon Kincaid* … and see how he eventually works it out! (56 Words)

A Race to a Death

Short Blurb: Walking on the 'wild side' was a way of life for *Indy racer Chuck Greene*. So why did he suddenly pack it all in and move to an isolated desert ranch with no electricity, no running water and no neighbours for fifty miles. Six months later, when they found his body, the mystery deepened as it came to light the last person to see him alive was on the *'Most Wanted' terrorist list in twenty three countries.* Hang on to your seats for a thriller ride of your life … with suspense in spades! (94 Words)

Single Sentence: The death of *Ex Indy racer, Chuck Greene* on his remote desert ranch and the unlikely connection with one of the *'Most Wanted' terrorists* in the world, kick-start a series of events that will possibly leave you gasping for breath! (40 Words)

The Eaton Affair

Short Blurb: Butter wouldn't melt in her mouth … they said. So what was she doing bending over the body of high *flying industrialist Marcus Eaton* … literally seconds after he had been fatally shot? The local police chief wanted to know and so did her *Langley boss at Section 'C', covert operations.* The problem is … no-one can find her. Has she disappeared out of choice or is there a more sinister reason? With a fast paced beginning, an explosive ending and a thriller of a tale between, *'The Eaton Affair'* makes compelling reading. (93 Words)

Single Sentence: A disciplined and experienced *female Section 'C' operative* caught bending over the dead body of a *wealthy, high flying industrialist* raises some questions at *Langley,* and ones that need answering … if they could only find her … and the reason for her worryingly sinister disappearance. (46 Words)

The Spanish Decision

Short Blurb: They were on *holiday in Spain* when it happened. A normal *American* family, enjoying their first taste of the fascinating *Spanish culture*, somehow get between the local police and two *bank robbers in*

Madrid. Adam Czerwinski, US citizen and father of two small adoring children has died in the cross fire … but who actually shot him? *Josi Czerwinski*, grieving wife and mother is determined to find out in the face of apathy, lies and deceit from all concerned. But is she getting in over her head? Is she about to blow a country-wide corruption scandal wide open? (97 Words)

Single Sentence: It's an unexpected outcome for the *Czerwinski* family, *holidaying in Spain* when father *Adam, a US citizen,* is fatally shot during a bank raid and his wife *Josi* is convinced that all is not as it should be with uncooperative police and threats to her life as she is about to blow open a country-wide corruption scandal. (57 Words)

Secrets of a Prodigal Son

Short Blurb: *Peter Wyndham* disappeared when he was *fourteen* years old. His parents searched and then grieved; their lives hollow and empty as they poured love enough for two onto their other child *Edmond. Fifteen years later, Peter* suddenly turns up on the doorstep of the *Wyndham* house in *Ohio,* with no recollection of where he's been or what he's been doing for all that time. *Edmond* does not believe it, the local police chief does not believe it … and most importantly, his mother does not believe it! When the truth is eventually revealed … it's a shocker! (97 Words)

Single Sentence: When *fourteen year old Peter Wyndham* completely disappears and then turns up *fifteen years later*, not knowing where he has been … not all are convinced, including the local police chief, his brother and his mother … who are simply unprepared for the shocking truth when it's finally revealed. (49 Words)

Political Thriller

The Downing Street Files

Short Blurb: *CIA Agent Levine* is sent to *10 Downing Street* on a routine security check ahead of a visit by the *US President.* He stumbles across an old file. Initially discussing this with the *British MI5 chief,* he knows nothing of its significance. The can of worms opens, sending *Levine* on the run, in strange territory, hunted by professionals and rejected by his own. He has uncovered minutes of a *1945 top secret meeting* between the wartime allies, the contents of which will create an International political explosion … if made public, bringing down governments. *Levine* however, has a different idea! (100 Words)

Single Sentence: An old, dusty file found in *10 Downing Street*, detailing the minutes of a top secret meeting of the *wartime allies in 1945*, sends *CIA Agent Levine* on the run in a strange country, hunted by professionals who wish to ensure the American security agent is silenced … not knowing a resourceful *Levine* has a somewhat different idea! (58 Words)

Politics of a Blackmailer

Short Blurb: A young *Senator,* an attractive *high class hooker* and the ambitions of a political adversary are not a good mix, especially when some embarrassing photographs turn up on *the Vice President's desk.* But is that all it is … just a bit of jealousy by a rival … or is there something much deeper involved, more complex and with much more serious consequences? What starts out as a simple bit of blackmail turns into an *International incident* … but who is really pulling all the strings … and more importantly, what is their real motive? (95 Words)

Single Sentence: When compromising images of a young *Senator* and a *high class hooker* turn up on the *Vice President's* desk, there could be several explanations, but what turns from a simple blackmail attempt into an *International* incident, leaves the *Presidency* reeling and someone in control with ambitions of a suspiciously dubious nature. (51 Words)

Death of a Diplomat's Daughter

Short Blurb: An election is due and all members of parliament must be on their best behaviour. So when the body of a *naked schoolgirl* is found in the *London apartment* of junior *Home Office minister Franklin,* his career looks to be at an end. But what is it that interests the *British SIS and American CIA?* She happens to be the daughter of a *top US diplomat* and the way she died causes some concern. Was *Franklin* responsible for her death … was he even seeing this young girl? He says 'NO' … but *CIA Agent Riggetti* is not convinced! (99 Words)

Single Sentence: The body of a *naked schoolgirl, daughter of a US Diplomat,* is discovered in the *London apartment of a UK junior Government Minister*, who denies all knowledge of her as *the British and American security services* get involved … and the convoluted path to the truth is gradually unravelled by a tenacious *CIA Agent Riggetti.* (55 Words)

Lying In State

Short Blurb: He was the *Governor* of a whole state … but not of his own life. *Ken Brewer* ruled that. He was the one who paid the bribes, the blackmail money and removed the drunken and drugged bodies of women from hotel rooms after the *sex crazed Governor* had finished with them. So … when *Brewer disappears*, the *Governor* is frantic to find him as his knowledge could put an end to an unsavoury political career. The mystery deepens as stories about the *Governor* begin to appear in national newspapers. He becomes desperate … and desperate men do desperate things! (99 Words)

Single Sentence: When *Ken Brewer,* a mister fix-it and minder to a *state Governor* disappears, a high power search is on as *Brewer* knows far too much … and of even more concern are stories that begin to circulate in the press about the *Governor* and the more hedonistic, or some might say … perverted side to his nature! (57 Words)

The Silent Scandal

Short Blurb: It was a mistake … and as soon as *White House Press Secretary Linda Carey* said it, she knew. They would pounce on it like a salivating pack of hungry hounds. *The President* would have to explain it himself now … and *Carey* would be out of a job. *The Russians* would take a dim view … the years of diplomatically good work done with them down the pan. But suddenly, everything went quiet. The *press* didn't mention it and neither did the *President.* Something was going on … and *Linda* was determined to get to the bottom of it. (100 Words)

Single Sentence: A massive political gaff made by *White House Press Secretary Linda Carey* leaves her fearing the worst, but strangely, there is no mention of it … by the *press* or the *White House* staff … and this leads *Linda* wondering why combined with a fearless determination to find out. (49 Words)

The Day They Lost Control

Short Blurb: It's all about *politics* … and that's how *Police Chief Masters* categorised all the bullshit that came down from the *Governor's* office. No one scored points against him for not doing his job … he wouldn't allow it, but moans and groans about parking tickets and underage drinking simply pissed him off … and he let them by. However, he would live to regret such a possibly careless attitude when one remarkably *simple parking ticket* situation began to turn into a national political scandal … over which he appeared to have no control! (93 Words)

Single Sentence: No one could possibly know that one *simple parking ticket* violation would turn into a national political scandal, least of all *Police Chief Masters* who needed to handle it … but it was getting away from him … and something drastic would have to happen if he was to survive the wounding ripple effect. (54 Words)

An Extraordinary History

Short Blurb: Its election time and *wealthy stockbroker Jason Burns* is up to take the vote for *US House of Representatives, New York District 27*. He is confident, has done his homework and greased a few relevant palms. But is it enough? He thinks so … until he starts receiving some mysterious and unwanted mail, making threats against his life unless he withdraws. With nowhere to turn, he eventually asks his friend *FBI Agent Tony Manchelli* to look into it. However, there are some frightening discoveries to contend with when uncovered and forgotten secrets in *Burns* past come back to haunt him. (100 Words)

Single Sentence: Asking a friend, *FBI Agent Tony Manchelli,* to look into disturbing mail being sent to wealthy stockbroker *Jason Burns,* just before his election to the *US House of Representatives*, was possibly a mistake when he uncovers some disturbingly deep, black shadows of a past that perhaps should have been left buried. (51 Words)

Step Back From the Brink

Short Blurb: It could be *nuclear war* … things were that bad. How they had reached this stage? *US President Reilly* didn't know … but he was sure of one thing, he needed some reliable intelligence from *Moscow* … and head of the *CIA, Robson Downey* assures him his best man is on the job. But when he surfaces head down in the *Volga, Downey* is out of answers and *Reilly* is out of time. One man in *Moscow,* however, knows what is happening by the hour and can keep *Reilly* up to date … but whose side is he really on? (100 Words)

Single Sentence: One agent dead in *Moscow* leaves *CIA Chief Downey* out of answers and *US President*

Reilly out of time in the intelligence game as the world teeters toward the brink of an all out *nuclear war* … until someone suddenly appears who seemingly knows what is happening inside the *Politburo*, but the big question is … which side is he really on? (62 Words)

The Gothenburg Papers

Short Blurb: 'He was caught with his trousers down'. That's the way the press handled it, but *British EU Member of Parliament Tony Stokes* knew there was more to the sex scandal he was now deeply bound up in than that. Firstly, he'd never met the girl involved; secondly the images the press had were fake, and thirdly he had never been in *Gothenburg* in his life. His quest for the truth reveals some murky links to the *Prime Minister's office* … and a set of right wing *Neo-Nazi* fanatics. Perhaps more than his political life could now be on the line? (100 Words)

Single Sentence: When *British EU Member of Parliament Tony Stokes* becomes embroiled in a sex scandal with a woman he has never met and faked images of him hitting the headlines, he embarks on a quest for the truth … unprepared for the revelations linked to the *Prime Minister's office* and a dangerous group of scheming *Neo-Nazi* fanatics! (56 Words)

The Death of a Healthy Man

Short Blurb: When healthy *Senator Hogarth* is struck down dead at a new-year party with close friends, the *FBI* initially suspect poison. *Pathologist Andy Cord* knows differently, but how to prove it. Within an hour of having *Hogarth* on the slab, he records traces of radio activity that two days later have gone. There are no untoward toxins in his body … no evidence of anything other than heart failure. *Cord* is not the kind of man to give in and when he ends up beaten half to death in the trunk of a crashed car … people start to listen. (99 Words)

Single Sentence: A healthy *Senator* struck down dead at a party and the suspicions of an investigating *Pathologist*, found beaten half to death in the trunk of a crashed car some days later, leave everyone in the world of high politics feeling insecure … when the real implications finally hit home! (49 Words)

Romance

A Love of Friends

Short Blurb: When *Janet* meets *Michael* for the first time, she is not impressed. However, a busy social calendar pursued against the backdrop of the *New York theatre scene* means they keep bumping into one another. Love comes upon them suddenly, fiercely, passionately … a painful kind of love that is destined not to last. However, when *Janet* thinks it's really all over … it is, until twenty years later when she opens the dating partner website *'Old Friends'*. Things will probably never be the same again. (85 Words)

Single Sentence: When *Janet* and *Michael* embark upon a passionate love affair … they both know that perhaps it's too good to last and so, twenty years later, when *Janet* opens the dating partner website *'Old Friends'*, she knows instinctively that things will probably never be the same again. (47 Words)

A Passionate Chase

Short Blurb: It was a *mid nineteenth century master* and *servant* relationship … or was it? How long would she take such verbal abuse from the man she hated but was bound to by family servitude? When she escaped, she thought he would not dare to come after her … but he did. Could such deep seated hate eventually turn to love? Will he be able to find her before she sinks into a life of *prostitution and physical neglect* … a life that could quickly be cut short by dramatically decaying health? Read it if you dare! (96 Words)

Single Sentence: In the *mid nineteenth century*, the relationship between *master and servant* was often one of verbal abuse and maltreatment, to the extent that one brave girl makes the decision to run … to escape, not thinking for one moment her *master* will come after her, seeking … and eventually finding her amongst a degenerate, low life society ruled by *physical abuse and prostitution.* (63 Words)

A Beautiful Entrapment

Short Blurb: She knew he was the one for her … the only one for her, from the very first time their eyes met. However, he was a married man, moving gradually up the social ladder to the heady heights of *Beverly Hills* high society. She was determined and within five years controlled her own highly successful *Los Angeles* business … a business looking for a new *corporate lawyer*. He got the job … now all she needed was his wife. All is fair in love and war … or so they say … and therefore the trap is finally set. (99 Words)

Single Sentence: He was the only one for her and she fought her way to the top of a tough *Los Angeles* business environment to have him … and now all she needed was to make his wife disappear! (37 Words)

Love in a Family Way

Short Blurb: When a confused and *depressed young girl* is re-united with her sisters, who she believed to have perished during the *Holocaust*, she will need to examine who she really is and whether or not the love she desperately seeks can be discovered through her new powers of communication. But can her physical lover ever become her true lover, or will the presence of her sisters create an unwelcome diversion. A story of deep feelings and emotions evoked by a need to be loved and a love to be needed … but in a way that that may shock and astonish! (100 Words)

Single Sentence: There's confusion aplenty in one *young girl's* disordered life when she discovers her sisters did not perish in the *Holocaust* and now, under their influence, she questions her relationship with a man who is her physical lover … but someone from who she wants much, much more! (47 Words)

A Self-indulgent Love

Short Blurb: In *eighteenth century New Orleans,* a haughty, proud and arrogant *Isabella*, the young and out of control daughter of wealthy *cotton plantation* owner *Silas Johnson,* comes to town looking for love … of a particular kind. However, she stumbles upon *Aaron*, a blond haired, fresh faced boy who she falls for at very first sight. They spend two wildly self-indulgent days together … but because of the substantial class difference between them, any ongoing relationship is doomed from the very start … or is it? Not if Isabella has her way. (91 Words)

Single Sentence: It's *eighteenth century New Orleans* and arrogant plantation owners daughter *Isabella* meets and falls for a young, fresh faced boy who joins her on a self indulgent affair that is not destined to last due to the substantial social gap in their lives … unless of course, a cunning *Isabella* has her way! (53 Words)

A French Inconvenience

Short Blurb: The boy next door becomes the love of *Sharon's* life and she is over the moon when he asks her to marry him. Life is bliss and with the addition of a beautiful child, the marriage appears to be a happy one. So, when tall, dark haired, good looking *Frenchman, Marcel* comes into her life, *Sharon* is unprepared for what happens next. She will need all her substantial willpower to keep confused physical feelings under control, desperately fighting the urge to betray her comfortable domestic situation. But will it be enough? (91 Words)

Single Sentence: A blissful marriage is about to be disturbed when *Sharon* meets charming *Frenchman Marcel* … and she is caught unprepared for what is about to happen, leaving her desperately fighting her physical feelings before her whole life spins violently out of control. (42 Words)

The Caribbean Option

Short Blurb: Three good looking women, all successful, well paid attorney's, on holiday in the exotic *Caribbean Island* of *Tobago*, are out for a good time … just a good time. So when local fisherman, *Moses Benson* makes a move on *Shirley*, she tells herself that fantastic sex is the singular driving force in their relationship. Ten days later, when it's time to go home, she is not so sure. Can *Shirley* ever consider giving up her first class lifestyle for a man … a man she has fallen in love with? That's one option … but is it the only one? (100 Words)

Single Sentence: Out of three, good looking successful single women on holiday together in exotic *Tobago*, *Shirley* is the one who falls for *Moses Benson* … telling herself it's a holiday romance, strong on sex and short on emotion, until it comes time to leave. (43 Words)

The Closeness of Love

Short Blurb: *She* never wanted it to happen, but it did. *He* sat next to her every day at work and they exchanged pleasantries on a regular basis. So, what went wrong? *He* didn't know either, but when he announced he was *leaving his wife* of six years for her, *she* was excited, bewildered and confused … all at the same time. *She* was sure of her love … but could she be sure of *him!* Would she simply accept that time would tell … or should she stop the *madness* right now! (91 Words)

Single Sentence: It wasn't bound to happen, but it did … when two work colleagues fall for one another with *him* announcing he is leaving *his wife* and her, knowing *she* was perhaps unsure of *him,* telling herself *she* should stop the madness … right now! (44 Words)

An Astonishing Relationship

Short Blurb: She knew what she wanted and she knew how to get it … from men anyway. So when her husband leaves her, unexpectedly, for another, younger version of herself, *Alice* is on a mission. *Walter,* a divorcee with custody of two problem children, does not appear to be a candidate for love, but when they bump into one another in a *supermarket* on a cold, wet *Saturday afternoon,* that was what they got. This often funny, sometimes poignant tale of love blossoming under the most difficult of circumstances, describes an astonishingly loving relationship, underscored by a spectacular romance. (98 Words)

Single Sentence: When her husband exits their marriage for a younger version of herself, *Alice* is on a mission and *Walter,* a divorcee with two problem children, becomes the focus of her attention in a story describing the growth of a spectacular love bound within an astonishingly moving romance. (48 Words)

The Familiar Stranger

Short Blurb: When the handsome and cavalier *Captain Smyth* goes to war, he leaves behind the beautiful, excitable eighteen year old *Lady Penelope Crowther* who is wealthy, single and in love. She promises to wait for him but fate dictates her gallant soldier will not return from the *1917* killing fields of *Passchendaele*. Ten years on, a stranger arrives at *Langley Hall,* the family seat of the Crowther family and causes an upset. Why is *Lady Penelope* so physically attracted to the stranger, a man who somehow looks so familiar? Has she denied herself love … for far too long? (98 Words)

Single Sentence: The killing fields of *Passchendale* in *1917* claim the life of the love of *Lady Penelope Crowther* and some ten years later is introduced to someone who is a stranger … but looks so damned familiar, leaving her confused with the unmistakable stirrings of a possible new love. (48 Words)

Science Fiction

Force From Within

Short Blurb: The crew of the *Universe Explorer* is *29 Astronomical Units* away from earth. There is a problem with the *Ion Drive* propulsion unit. Without it there will be no electrical power. Someone suspects sabotage but a decision must be made by *Captain Senoko* as to whether to turn back … or carry on their mission … out of the *Solar System.* Then, one after the other, the ship's systems all shut down. What is the strange, intelligent force acting on them and who is controlling it? Time is on no one's side! (92 Words)

Single Sentence: What or who is behind the series of misfortunes plaguing the star ship *Universe Explorer* making some suspect sabotage and urging *Captain Senoko* to make a decision to turn back … before they eject out of the *Solar System* on a mission … with some form of strange, intelligent force acting upon them! (53 Words)

The Deadly Decision

Short Blurb: When *biological warfare* specialist *Dr Dan Powers* is pulled from retirement, he knows something big is going down. A master of *chemical formulation*, even he is unprepared for what happens next as a *deadly virus* combines with the very latest 21st Century *Nano technology* to produce a weapon capable of unbelievable destruction. There is no antidote, there is no defence, there is no time to find one … but is there? Only *Powers* believes there is … if he can live long enough to prove it? (86 Words)

Single Sentence: When *biological warfare* specialist *Dr Dan Powers* is pulled from retirement to investigate the unstoppable propagation of a deadly *chemical weapon*, he is told there is no antidote, no defence and no time … unless, of course, he can live long enough find one! (44 Words)

Treasure on Earth

Short Blurb: On *Artemius* there is a crisis. Life sustaining water is rapidly running out. Another source must be found … and quickly. The *Inter Galactic* research ship *Tyronius III* is sent out to look for it. By marshalling hundreds of sensing robot craft ahead, crew learn from the retrieved data about a blue planet in a small and distant solar system, literally covered in what appears to be water. With a course set at full speed, the *Tyronious* heads for the mysterious planet … but what kind of reception will they get from the life saving blue planet called *'Earth'*? (99 Words)

Single Sentence: When the planet *Artemius* is about to run out of life sustaining water, an *Inter Galactic* research ship is sent to find some … and heads for a blue planet, the planet Earth … but what kind of reception will they get? (41 Words)

The Amoeba Theory

Short Blurb: It started out as a *modified single cell amoeba*, but no one could possibly conceive what was to come next. *Doctor Margret Allenby* knew the answer to the problem, but would anyone listen? At the secret *US Green Lake* research facility, things were getting out of control, possibly threatening the security of a nation … if not the world. *The President* would need to be told … unless of course it was already too late! (75 Words)

Single Sentence: What started out as a *single cell amoeba* being modified at a *secret US chemical research* facility turned into a nightmare, out of control project threatening the security of a nation … if not the world … and someone needed to tell *the President!* (44 Words)

An Ancient Lethal Burial

Short Blurb: The discovery by the *US research team* was hailed as the most important archaeological project of the century … but had something less savoury been unearthed in the process. People started dying … in larger and larger numbers until the whole of the *Argentinean* site had to be quarantined. What was the mystery attached to the *10,000 year old statues?* Who made them and what did they represent? If the sickening body count was anything to go by, there was an evil presence here with an influence on human life never, ever seen or recorded on earth before! (98 Words)

Single Sentence: A ten thousand year old archaeological discovery in *Argentina* is linked to a series of unexplained deaths with some coming to believe an evil presence has been released, never seen or recorded before on earth … and the sickening body count is growing! (43 Words)

Zero Defence

Short Blurb: When a massive *Electro Magnetic Pulse* sweeps round the world carrying with it electrical energy strong enough to wipe out the Earth's communication systems, the question needs asking … 'where the hell has it come from?' *US President A.R. Withens* requires an answer amongst sombre predictions it would take two years to get the world's major microwave systems up and running again. Who was now the enemy of a near defenceless *America?* Perhaps such an enemy was more capable and possibly much closer than most would dare to believe? (89 Words)

Single Sentence: With the world's electronic communications systems stunned by a massive *Electro Magnetic Pulse* … and a prediction it will take two years to get them all up and running again, *US President A.R Withens* wants an answer to the question a now defenceless *America* is asking … 'where the hell did it come from?' (54 Words)

A Deep Discovery

Short Blurb: One determined, highly qualified marine engineer leads a team of equally resolute scientists on a mission to recover a crashed space-craft, carrying a quantity of *bacteria* samples from a distant galaxy. It's resting thousands of feet deep on the *Pacific Ocean* floor. They eventually find and recover it and all seems well until the second night on board the recovery vessel when strange things start to occur. With the ships compass showing one direction but the vessel going in another, the crew appear to have lost control. Someone … or something has taken over, pushing them toward a mysterious destination! (100 Words)

Single Sentence: A crashed space craft carrying stellar *bacteria* samples; recovery from the depths of the *Pacific Ocean* and a research vessel taken over by some mysterious force leaves a team of experienced on-board scientists and marine engineers baffled … and fearful for their future! (43 Words)

The Kidnapping of Joanna Woolly

Short Blurb: She was only a child … but what could she see that others couldn't? Was it genuine talent or a trick perpetrated by manipulating parents? Some didn't think so and the unsolved kidnapping of *Joanna Woolly* became a major incident for the *Texas* town of *Phillimore*. Ten years later a young psychic named *Anastacia* bursts upon *America.* She foretells events happening only weeks ahead and millions follow on the promise they will be taken up to a new life on a new planet as the life support systems on *Earth* slowly disintegrate. What will happen when the panic sets in? (100 Words)

Single Sentence: Ten years after an unsolved kidnapping of a mystic child in the sleepy *Texas* town of *Phillimore,* a young psychic, calling herself *Anastacia,* bursts upon an unprepared *America,* foretelling events weeks ahead on earth and offering a new life … on a new planet, but not knowing what will happen when the panic sets in! (55 Words)

The Communicators

Short Blurb: At the beginning of *Century Twenty Three,* mind over matter was a well practiced art that some were better at than others. However, one man not only wanted to control matter with his mind, he wanted to control the minds of others as well. His determination to practice his skill for financial gain brought him great riches … until … one day, someone would come into his life to change all that. The battle of two superior minds would begin, but who would prevail … and what or who would need to be destroyed in the process? (97 Words)

Single Sentence: In *Century Twenty Three,* well practiced 'mind over matter' brought one man great riches, controlling the minds of others, until one day, he would meet his match … and the battle would begin, not knowing what or who would need to be destroyed in the process of claiming victory. (49 Words)

A Disquieting Discovery

Short Blurb: Why had the *Soviet Zukov Class nuclear submarine*, on normal patrol duties, disappeared from waters close to the US Eastern seaboard? It remained a mystery until seven years later a British research deep diving bell discovered the wreckage. Unusual hull damage indicated the submarine had been literally battered to a pulp by something … something very large and very vicious … but what? Captain Willoughby of the research ship 'Sea Pride' was about to find out. But this would not be the end of it! (85 Words)

Single Sentence: With discovery of the mysteriously battered wreckage of a *Soviet submarine*, *Captain*

Willoughby … in charge of the research vessel *'Sea Pride'* has his concerns … and ones that will shortly turn into an horrific and frightening reality … but that would not be the end of it! (48 Words)

War

Diary of a Dead Man

Short Blurb: They had taken the same piece of land fourteen times in the past six weeks and in the doing had lost over a hundred men. The *trenches of northern France*, in the winter of *1916,* were not the place to be, by *Corporal Evans* reckoning … and he planned to remove himself from his displeasing situation very shortly. Describing in fascinating detail the following twelve weeks of *Evans* life on the mud caked *battle fields of Europe* will leave the reader amused, sometimes shocked and often reflective about the reality of war and its unwilling participants. (96 Words)

Single Sentence: This is a sometimes shocking … sometimes amusing story of one man and his relentless efforts to remove himself from the unhealthy lifestyle of the *northern French trenches* in *1916* … describing in fascinating detail what happens over a period of twelve short weeks. (44 Words)

Lost Mission in Laos

Short Blurb: *Ranger Captain Chuck Bradley* leads his small group of men cautiously through the thick jungle of what is *Laos.* Why are they there … because the *Ho Chi Minh trail* is there? It's *February, 1971.* A decision is made to cut the trail. *Bradley* and his men are designated as the forward intelligence unit … but the ill-conceived mission comes to an abrupt end when two of his men are killed in a poison stake trap. Someone will have to pay, but *Bradley* will need to get his men out of the clutches of a sadistic *Viet Cong General* first! (100 Words)

Single Sentence: When *Ranger Captain Chuck Bradley* accepts a mission to cut the *Ho Chi Minh trail* in *Laos*, he is concerned the mission is ill-conceived, but when he loses two men in an ugly poison trap and falls into the clutches of a sadistic Viet Cong General … he knows he has a job on his hands! (56 Words)

Tracked

Short Blurb: *Squadron commander Ryan Strong* knew the *Iraqis* were in front of him as he gave the order to start up his tanks on that damp, *desert* morning. It would be hot soon; he needed to be at his firing point within the hour. The platoon of battle hardened, *Iraqi Presidential Guard* behind him had other ideas as one by one, *Ryan's* tanks and their crews disappeared in explosive balls of flame, leaving black smoked, twisted tombstone wreckage behind. There could only be one winner in what was now a personal war … all dependent upon who blinked first! (98 Words)

Single Sentence: As *tank squadron commander Ryan Strong* began losing his tanks and crews in the arid *Iraqi desert* to a well trained enemy behind him, the whole deal became personal … and the winner would definitely not be the one who blinked first. (42 Words)

The Great French Evasion

Short Blurb: Fifteen men wearing *red beret's* … the green light, the anticipated tap on the shoulder and one by one jumping out of the unlit *DC3* into pitch black darkness over *France.* Huddled together, exposed in the middle of a muddy ploughed field, their worst fears were confirmed. They were over thirty miles away from their mission drop zone … and from the noise and lights on the horizon, the *Germans* were coming. This is the fascinating and gripping story of what happened next and how every single man survived, escaped *France* and made their way back to a welcoming *England.* (100 Words)

Single Sentence: The fifteen *red beret's* that parachuted into *France* on that pitch black, chilling night, found themselves many miles from their drop zone … and *Germans* too close for comfort, leaving them no choice but to escape France and get back to besieged England … but that would not be without its problems! (52 Words)

Death of a Code Breaker

Short Blurb: 'Wars are very rarely won on the field of battle' … advised *Major Curtiss*. He of course has an axe to grind as officer in charge of *'Section H' at Bletchley Park* and is convinced the secret to winning a war is knowing the other side's secrets. *Curtiss* is an ace code-breaker and *Julia,* a *Cambridge Maths First,* joining his section that day, found it hard to suppress her excitement. Perhaps she should have waited; three weeks later she would be dead. Who did it … and why? The winning or otherwise of *World War II* was possibly at stake! (100 Words)

Single Sentence: At the top secret code breaking center of *Bletchley Park, England*, *Julia* joins the hi-power team but is dead three weeks later, leaving a secret for the code breakers to unravel before it's too late … and *World War II* is possibly lost! (42 Words)

The Trail of a Traitor

Short Blurb: They have guns … he has a knife; but that is no problem to *Special Forces Sergeant Bikerslow.* He will take out the *Viet Cong* patrols guarding the makeshift prison camp at *Dho Chi,* silently … then carve a way in for those behind him. Twenty beaten and badly treated *US Marines* are relying on him. Suddenly, the world lights up around him. Something has gone dramatically wrong. Someone has been betrayed! *Bikerslow* will survive … just, but he will spend the next twenty years finding out who it was … and considering how slowly their life will eventually end. (100 Words)

Single Sentence: Being betrayed breaking into the notorious *Viet Cong* prison camp at *Dho Chi, Special Forces Sergeant Bikerslow* will survive … just, but he will also spend the next twenty years finding out who the vile deceiver really was … and considering how painfully he must eventually die! (47 Words)

The Deceitful Diaries of Corporal Timms

Short Blurb: They were diaries, a collection of scribbles on odd bits of paper … or so he said. They described three years of life in the trenches from *1916 to 1918* … but no one thought they would become a best seller, projecting *ex-corporal Timms* to literary stardom. However, when *Tommy Dickson* reads them, he realizes the diaries are not *Timms'* experiences … but his! The two men come face to face. Can *Timms* prove the diaries belong to him? In a final, unexpected twist, *Dickson* realises this man is not actually *Timms* at all. So who is he? (98 Words)

Single Sentence: A writer of wartime diaries becomes an overnight success when his words are published, but someone else recognizes them as his own and when they meet, face to face, in an unexpected twist, one of them appears not to be who he claims … so who on earth is he? (50 Words)

Escape of the Eagles

Short Blurb: He was a fighter ace; twelve *German* aircraft shot down in seven months. In *1941, US Captain Granger* flying with one of the *British Air Force 'Eagle Squadrons'* was due a rest. He took comfort in the news that *America* would join the war in *Europe* shortly and then he could fly under a *US command.* However, fate dictated otherwise when he was shot down over *France*, spending the next four years organising escape routes for *US airmen into Spain.* This is a story of courage, commitment and sometimes bloody mindedness in a man who only knew how to win. (100 Words)

Single Sentence: *US fighter pilot Captain Granger* is looking forward to flying under a *US command* but is shot down over *France in 1941* where, for the next four years he organises escape routes *for US airmen* into *Spain* in a superb tale of courage, commitment and sometimes outright bloody mindedness. (49 Words)

He Who Shoots Last …

Short Blurb: *US Submarine Cuttlefish* had two torpedoes left and the *Japanese* fast frigate racing through the water sixty feet above it had the boat locked in on sonar. There was only one thing for it … hit the bottom. *Commander Jeff Stanton* knew how to play a waiting game but didn't account for a rogue depth charge that literally blew the steering gear to pieces and set the boat on an upward journey. Could a surfaced, un-steerable submarine outgun a frigate? *Commander Stanton* was about to find out! (87 Words)

Single Sentence: When *US Submarine Cuttlefish* loses its steering gear in a depth charge attack and his boat is heading uncontrollably to the surface, *Commander Jeff Stanton* ponders on the possibility of an un-steerable submarine outgunning a Japanese frigate on the surface … knowing he is about to find out! (48 Words)

The Gold Chasers

Short Blurb: It's gold they're chasing. *Nazi gold …* and by the time the troop of thirty *US Marines* have fought their way to the gates of *Kronig Castle,* they know it's not far away. The *Germans* are retreating left, right and centre in front of them … but the *SS Troops* guarding *Hitler's booty*, behind the sturdy castle walls, are not. This is a dilemma *for Major Hawkins* and one he didn't have an immediate answer to. What happens next is a story of some courage, a little foolishness, a lot of confidence and perhaps eventually too much reliance upon luck. (100 Words)

Single Sentence: In a desperate chase across war torn *Germany* to find a large consignment of *Nazi gold*, *Major Hawkins* and his group of *US Marines* end up at *Kronig Castle,* facing *determined SS Troops* … and although this was not what the Major was expecting, what happens next makes this a gripping tale of mixed fortunes. (55 Words)

Women's Fiction

A Burial in Nantes

Short Blurb: When *Jane* discovers her older sister is actually her half-sister, she desperately wants to find out why her parents had never divulged such a heartbreakingly important fact to her. She is hurt and confused, but would delving into the past of her long deceased mother provide any of the answers she is looking for. *Jane* embarks on a journey taking her back to the *Second World War*, the *French Resistance* and a mysterious *American OSS Officer* buried in a graveyard in *Nantes.* She will need to steel herself for the truth ... if indeed she is ready to receive it! (100 Words)

Single Sentence: Discovering her older sister is in fact her half sister sends *Jane* on a painful journey through her mother's past, back to the *Second World War*, a mysterious *American OSS Officer* and the *French Resistance* ... concluding in a set of possibly disassembled truths she may not be emotionally ready to receive. (52 Words)

Changing Spaces

Short Blurb: When three good friends, three hardworking homemakers, three attractive women … all arrange for a night out in *New York.* What could possibly go wrong? That's the singular and most important question each one knows they should have asked themselves as they wake up the following day to discover their lives have changed completely … and forever, in a gripping story of passion, grief and personal discovery. (67 Words)

Single Sentence: When three hardworking, attractive women go out for a night on the town in *New York,* they wake up the following day to find their lives have changed … beyond comprehension, leaving them to battle with the passions, grief and personal discovery associated with their strange new world. (48 Words)

A Woman with a Warning

Short Blurb: Attractive, ambitious and well educated *Celia Southern* was at the bottom. She needed to be at the top. It was that simple. But getting there would involve embarking on a plan to take out the uninspiring and unsuspecting male obstacles in her path. Using her subtle charm, her obvious intellect and exceptional looks to rise to the very top of her profession … once she gets there *Celia* is left feeling lonely and unfulfilled. Then … handsome, fit and refreshingly intelligent *Jonathan Ridgeway* appears on the scene … and all bets are suddenly off! (94 Words)

Single Sentence: Having battled her way to the top, exceptionally attractive and intelligent *Celia Southern* is left feeling lonely and unfulfilled … until the handsome, intelligent and very fit looking *Jonathan Ridgeway* appears on the scene … and now the games can begin! (41 Words)

Fatal Love

Short Blurb: This is the disturbing story of a mother and her son … a drug addict; a young hopelessly insecure individual who robs and steals from her on a daily basis. However, one day *Amber Johnson* decides enough is enough and the emotional shutters come down. Armed with a strong will, three months leave from her job and a *.45 automatic, Amber* sets out to find the low life scum feeding her son's drug habit … and when that happens, all hell breaks loose! (83 Words)

Single Sentence: When caring mother, *Amber Johnson* decides not to take any more physical and mental abuse from her drug addicted son, the shutters come down and armed with a *.45 automatic* and three weeks leave from her job, she sets out to find the low life scum who set her son on his path of madness …

and when she finds them, all hell breaks loose! (65 Words)

Trouble to Translate

Short Blurb: Winter in *Moscow* was not part of the plan, but the services of thirty three year old *diplomatic translator Irene Weisman* were required by *US Ambassador Rickman* … and questioning such a request was not an option. So would it have all happened if she had said no? This life changing decision had left her beaten and bruised, unable to think coherently and locked in a freezing, bare walled, window barred room, literally wondering what was the hell happening. Perhaps *Ambassador Rickman* would be able to tell her … if they only knew where he was? (96 Words)

Single Sentence: When the services of *diplomatic translator Irene Weisman* were demanded *by US Ambassador Rickman,* in a wintery cold war Moscow, little did she expect to end up physically beaten and imprisoned as part of an incomprehensible set of circumstances that only the *Ambassador* could explain … that is of course … if they knew where the hell he was? (59 Words)

The Thornberry Seduction

Short Blurb: In *19th Century Boston*, one woman's resolve could be the undoing of another. So, when

Jessica Reynolds comes face to face with the *English visitor, Lady Maria Thornberry*, everyone in the *Reynolds* family prepares for the sparks to fly. At the centre of it all is a man; a very special kind of man, a man *Jessica* is due to marry … a man about to receive a substantial dowry from *Jessica's* father. *Lady Maria* however, has a different ambition … and things are necessarily bound to become complicated! (89 Words)

Single Sentence: When *19th Century Boston* society receives well connected *English visitor Lady Maria Thornberry,* the recently engaged *Jessica Reynolds* is protective of her future husband and sparks begin to fly as *Lady Maria* seems to have other ambitions for the attractive young man … making things quite necessarily complicated. (48 Words)

A Trip to Confinement

Short Blurb: One outwardly happy young girl with two stable men in her life is working hard to build her own small *vintage fashion* business. All she needs is an extra *$10,000* to set up shop with a new line of stock … moving her into the big-time. One quick trip to *Venezuela* would do the job. She knew it was true … her best friend had told her so! However, when the friendly looking little dog began to sniff her luggage at *Caracas* airport … her life was about to change forever. This is her story! (95 Words)

Single Sentence: When a sensible, well grounded but ambitious girl, with her own successful *vintage fashion* business finds herself at *Venezuela's Caracas* airport, with a drug sniffer dog paying her much more attention that he should … her life is about to change forever … and this is her harrowing story. (49 Words)

A Game for Girls

Short Blurb: Two attractive women, friends since high school, chasing the same man … leaves little room for manoeuvre … until the man in question disappears, unexpectedly out of their lives. The choice is forget him … or find him, but they will both need a little help with the latter. *Private Detective Charlie Burton* arrives on the scene and with his help they are expecting a result … but what kind of result? The more he delves into the past life of the 'missing person', the more he uncovers mysterious links to his two employers. Someone is playing games! (98 Words)

Single Sentence: Two attractive women chasing one attractive man could be a sign of trouble … until he disappears and private *Detective Charlie Burton* is asked to find him, with some unexpected results and a suspicion that someone maybe playing a dangerous game! (41 Words)

When the Fast Lady Stops

Short Blurb: It was a *finishing school* for ladies, but one lady in particular was more than finished when she left there. In fact the *Honourable Felicity Grey* knew how to pick a lock, drive a fast car, shuffle a pack of cards … so an ace always came on top … and seduce just about anything in trousers. The *scam* was a good one, she was bound to come out ahead, but nobody told her what would happen if she didn't. When she found out, it would probably be too damn late! (91 Words)

Single Sentence: When the *Honourable Felicity Grey* walked out of *'finishing school'* she was confident she knew more than she should about criminality and seduction … but such confidence could be her undoing in a *scam* that looked as if it was going wrong … and now it was too damn late! (50 Words)

Ghosts from a Distant Childhood

Short Blurb: They were *sisters* … and had not seen one another for years. When they eventually met, there was an uncomfortable distance between them; a distance unable to be lessened until the truth was aired surrounding an event that had happened thirty years previously. Some unbidden ghosts from a *troubled childhood* would haunt their conversation until it was all out … but what would happen then? (65 Words)

Single Sentence: Two *sisters*, meeting for the first time after many years need to have a conversation to lay down some ghosts from a *troubled childhood* … but when they do what happens afterwards? (32 Words)

Pursued

Short Blurb: She was betrothed to a difficult man. Twenty years on from a 1960's marriage and a nineteen year old son at university, Peggy Richmond was prepared to make a move; change her drudge of a life for the better. When she finally made the decision, he would not be pleased; in fact he would pursue her, relentlessly until finally, she had to give in, triggering a set of events that would scar her life forever. When the bombshell burst, the emotional shrapnel would spread far and wide … and at least one person was unprepared for the substantial fallout. (99 Words)

Single Sentence: Peggy Richmond's life was a drudge married to a most difficult man and she needed to change it, but when she did, he pursued her relentlessly until she could take no more … and then the inevitable explosion happened … with some unprepared for the sizeable fallout! (47 Words)

The Full Blurb Tips

The Full Blurb:

The 'full' blurb, being a distillation of the synopsis, will by necessity end up as a quite intense description of the action taking place in a manuscript and a much condensed view of the key characters. With even a refined synopsis still weighing in at a full page or two, a full blurb should be less than a page and possibly no more than half a page. Ideally, it will be the right size to fill the rear of the cover jacket if you are producing for print and end up at approximately 200 or 300 finished words. It will need to be punchy, truthful (no embellishments of people or situations that are not actually contained within the manuscript) and descriptive, providing tension and delivering the obvious question of 'what happens next?' for thriller writers. Below are two examples from some of this author's published novels with the first example being a women's fiction thriller simply but intriguingly entitled – 'Rosalind'.

Para 1 describing the beginning of the story:

When a stunningly beautiful, sexually aware woman and escape from a violent, abusive father combine with a new life in the big city, they make the story of Rosalind one of strength and determination in a quest to conquer her past.

Para 2 describing the middle of the story:

A change of name completes her transformation in to a new woman, one who is swept off her feet by a handsome, staggeringly rich Arab Prince. But being isolated and then imprisoned in a desert Sheikdom, forced in to sexual slavery and foiled in her attempt to escape, leads to unexpected violence and a possible cover-up.

Para 3 describing the end of the story:

Her friend in New York is distraught and vows to confront the powerful, diplomatically protected Arab multi millionaire to get at the truth. The ultimate encounter between one frighteningly resolute woman and the politically astute, influential, Arab Prince leaves a scene of carnage, as in the final account, only one person can walk away. But will there be more than one survivor, and who could it possibly be?

Para 4 describing the setting of the story:

Set in the world financial depression of the 1970's, this is the sometimes heartbreaking story of powerfully portrayed characters that will become more and more a part of you with every turn of the page.

This full blurb is exactly 200 words long and as indicated, is divided into four paragraphs. The first three simply indicate the beginning, middle and end of the story and the final paragraph defines the setting of the story and a hint at the characterization involved.

Now, the Short Blurb:

As we said at the beginning, the 'short' blurb is a further distillation of the full blurb and will need to sum up the plot and main characters in short, explosive sentences. Here's an example taken from the descriptive information contained in the 'full blurb' above.

Its 1970's America and a quest for sexual fulfillment leads Rosalind into the clutches of a deceitful Arab Prince. Forced into degrading sexual slavery in the overheated climate of a distant desert Sheikdom ... could this be the end? (39 Words)

However, justice must be done in this powerful thriller, about strong minded women in a tough man's world of unbelievable riches and privilege ... where survival is the only goal. (30 Words)

Total: 67 Words

This short blurb has taken the complete synopsis from over 800 words down to the full blurb of 200 words and now significantly less than 100 words. Finally, below is an even shorter distillation ending up as one single sentence blurb for the same storyline.

The deceiving affections of an Arabian Prince, sexual slavery, and a disturbing retribution: from the very start, two strong female characters are brought vibrantly alive in this thriller with a unique twist in the tail.

Total 35 Words

Another Example:

Below is a second and final example from another one of this author's published novels, a techno-thriller descriptively entitled – 'The Ludlum Prediction'.

Para 1 describing the beginning of the story:

It's the year 2018. North Platte, Lincoln County is a place noted for declining employment prospects at the once famous railroad depot ... and little else. For Ed Ludlum, he could reside anywhere and still earn a good living as a 'Data Miner' ... someone who cannot only tell you what you'll shop for next Wednesday at three o'clock, but which shop you'll use ... and what shelf you'll find it on.

Para 2 describing the background to the story and introducing one of the major players:

However, a powerful, wealthy and well connected US based secretive religious sect, the Messianic Tribes of Yashoa, known by many simply as the MTY, wish to avail themselves of Ed Ludlum's unique services ... and they are willing to pay well for it. They want to extract a date and a place from hundreds of terabytes of data, collected over many years from the darkest depths of some ancient sciences and leftover mysterious hieroglyphs, abandoned by long lost civilizations. But what is all this high tech computer based research for?

Para 3 describing the hook to the story and introducing the other major players:

The work of Ed Ludlum soon comes to the attention of some of the most powerful Intelligence Agencies in the world, such as the CIA, the British SIS and the much feared Israeli Mossad, becoming known as 'The Ludlum Prediction' ... a prophesy that if fulfilled, could possibly change the world as we know it ... forever!

Para 4 describing the lead-in to the main plot:

Sitting on the sidelines, surrounded by Vatican based Cardinals whose common survival plan is based on ignorance and self serving edicts, is one man with the power and determination to thwart the best laid plans of highly professional State Intelligence Agents. He knows that if 'The Ludlum Prediction' is in any way linked to the expected appearance of a new prophet, or religious deity, then the Catholic Church could be led to the edge of a credibility precipice.

Para 5 describing an unexpected change of direction in the story line:

Has Ed Ludlum got it right? With the surprise discovery of 3000 year old tablets linking two great civilizations and key religious beliefs together ... half a world apart ... he thinks he has. However, the very best of carefully executed plans can fail, as they did, so horrifically in the chilling final hours of what was to be the end game adventure, played out on a remote Tibetan plateau ... only miles from the militarily sensitive Chinese border.

Para 6 raising questions of doubt:

Will this bring an end to all the speculation and questions of legitimacy surrounding 'The Ludlum Prediction', or trigger a new series of events that could inevitably lead to the beginning of a new world crisis?

Para 7 leaving the reader to ponder the actual outcome:

Perhaps there is something even more sinister afoot, urging Ludlum down a path ... to a place ... from which there will be no possible return! Could 'The Ludlum Prediction' in fact be reality? Is it about to happen ... or, more concerning for some ... could it have happened already?

You decide..!

Total: 465 Words

Now, the Short Blurb:

So, here's the second example taken from the descriptive information contained in the 'full blurb' above.

One man, one super computer, a determined powerful religious sect and the limitless resources of some of the world's biggest intelligence agencies, combine to pursue what has become known as 'The Ludlum Prediction'. Is this a prophetic event ... a second coming ... and if so ... the second coming of what? Could it really happen ... has it already happened and are we living with its consequences right now? Only you can decide the worth of the evidence and confirm your belief or non-belief in 'The Ludlum Prediction'.

Total: 89 Words

This short blurb has taken the original already compressed synopsis from over 400 words down to a short blurb of less than 90 words. Below is the shorter distillation ending up as one single sentence blurb for exactly the same storyline.

One man and a super computer, with a determined powerful religious sect on his tail and 'The Ludlum Prediction' is born ... but is this a prophetic event ... a second coming ... and if so ... the second coming of what?

Total: 42 Words

Blurb Importance:

Finally, as stated previously, the combination of 'blurb' and 'cover image' are really at the heart of how successfully you will be able to market your book to potential readers. In effect, the blurb is the key element of tempting the reader to open the very first page. The cover image is designed to attract attention, but it is the blurb that actually advertises to the reader, what might be between the covers. There is a popular saying in the world of commercial advertising that goes like this.
"Good advertising can clear shelves; great advertising can build factories ..!"
So, you need to spend some time on getting your 'blurb' right … it is your single 'advertising' opportunity at your point of sale … and can perhaps

'allow you to build factories'! Don't forget to 'distill' with care, making sure the key elements of your story remain after a final fierce edit. Get some other opinions on your final blurb. Ask friends to read it and tell you honestly if such a 'hook' would persuade them to buy the actual product.

THE END

www.quentincope.co.uk

Made in the USA
San Bernardino, CA
24 January 2016